Famous Scientific Procedures

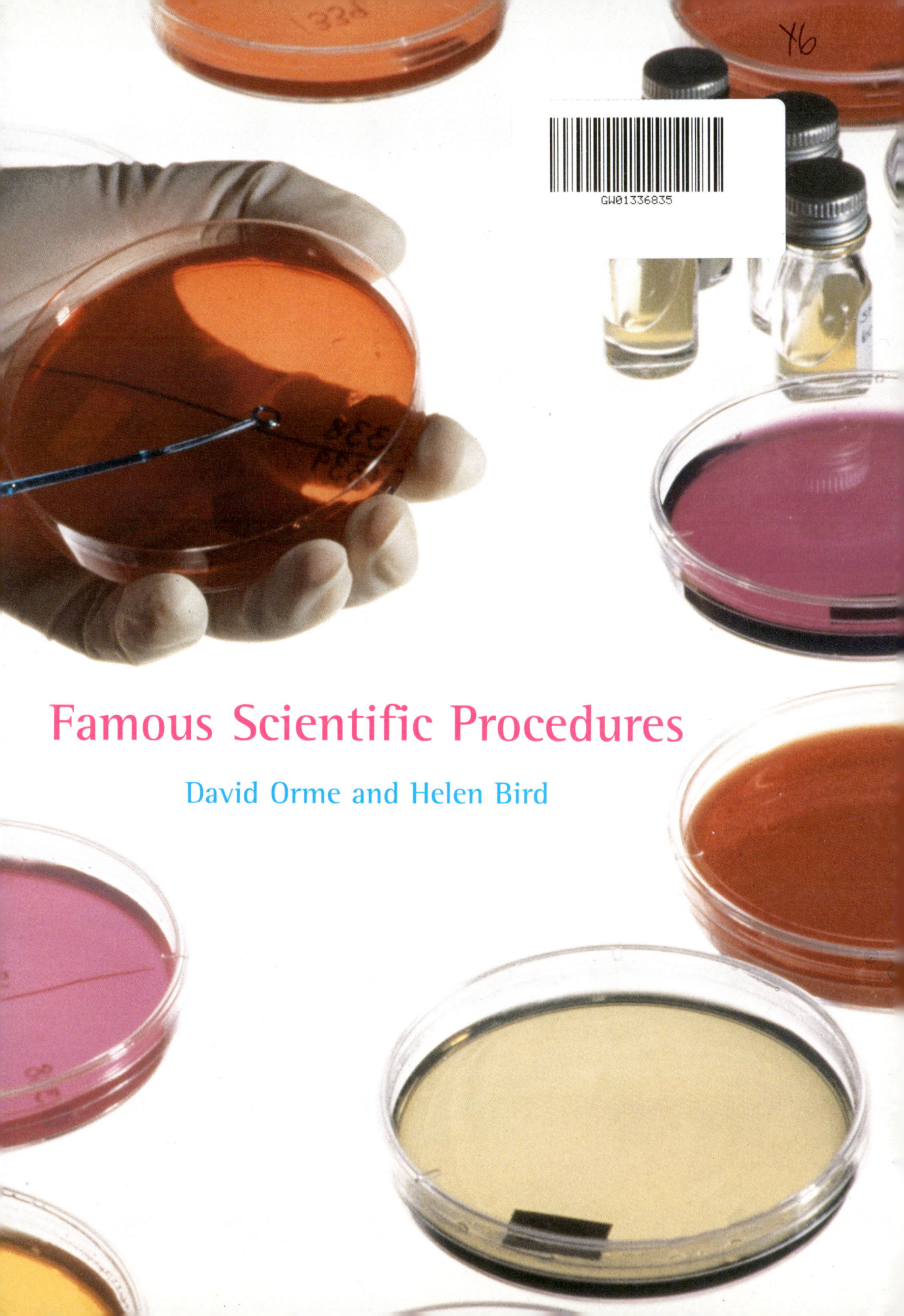

David Orme and Helen Bird

Published by HarperCollins*Publishers* Ltd
77–85 Fulham Palace Road
Hammersmith
London
W6 8JB

www.CollinsEducation.com
Online support for schools and colleges

© HarperCollins*Publishers* Limited 2002

First published 2002

Reprinted 10 9 8 7 6 5 4 3 2 1

ISBN 0 00 713837 7

David Orme and Helen Bird assert the moral right to be identified as the authors of this work.

All rights reserved. No part of this publication may be reproduced, stored in a retrieval system, or transmitted in any form or by any other means, electronic, mechanical, photocopying, recording or otherwise, without either the prior permission of the Publisher or a licence permitting restricted copying in the United Kingdom issued by the Copyright Licensing Agency Ltd., 90 Tottenham Court Road, London W1P 9HE.

British Library Cataloguing in Publication Data
A Catalogue record for this publication is available from the British Library

Series editor: Maureen Lewis
Creative director: Louise Morley
Designers: Celia Hart and Sarah Christie
Editor: Jo Kemp
Cover photographs: Mary Evans Picture Library: Sir Alexander Fleming; Science Photo Library: notes on and a drawing of the original culture plate of the fungus penicillium notatum, Bikini Atoll detonation of an atomic bomb, Sellafield nuclear power plant.
Illustrations: Ian Hunt
Photographs: Steve Lumb Photography pp.5BL, 12, 13, 17, 20, 29, 30
The publishers would like to thank Comber Grove Primary School, Camberwell, London for their participation

The publishers wish to thank the following for permission to use photographs:
Science Photo Library pp.1, 5R, 7, 8T, 9, 11, 14, 16, 18, 19, 21, 23TR, 24, 25, 27, 28;
John Walmsley p.5 BL; Mary Evans Picture Library pp.6, 8BR, 10, 22, 23BL

Every effort has been made to trace copyright holders and to obtain their permission for the use of copyright material. The author and publishers will gladly receive any information enabling them to rectify any error or omission in subsequent editions.

Printed by: Printing Express Ltd, Hong Kong

You might also like to visit
www.fireandwater.co.uk
The book lover's website

Contents

Introduction   5

Mysterious moulds   6

How heavy   14

Radioactive reactions   22

Glossary   31

Index   32

Introduction

All scientists learn how to do some basic scientific procedures that they will use again and again in their work. These might include changing materials through heat, mixing materials together, separating materials from each other, or weighing and measuring objects. These procedures are repeated many times to test that the results are consistent. They are important because they can be used in many ways and can be modified for different problems.

As you read this book you will learn how great scientific discoveries arose from, or were confirmed by, some basic scientific procedures – growing things in a particular environment, investigating forces by observing objects as they fall, and separating materials from each other.

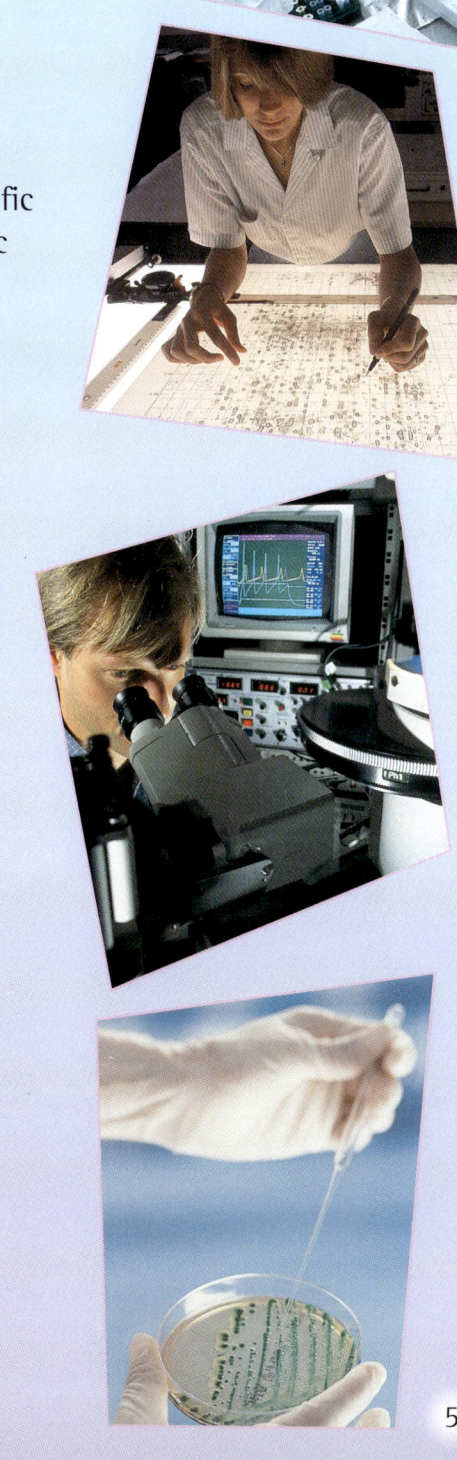

Mysterious moulds

Before the discovery of **antibiotics**, infections caused by **bacteria** were a major problem – even minor wounds could turn **septic** and lead to death. In wartime, many more soldiers died from infection than were killed on the battlefield. At this time, too, there was little that could be done to cure a whole range of diseases such as diphtheria and typhoid. By the end of the 19th century, it was well known that these diseases and infections were caused by bacteria, but no one knew how they could be defeated.

Throughout the 1920s, 1930s and 1940s, experiments were conducted and discoveries made that would change the world of medicine forever. A British scientist, Alexander Fleming, made the initial findings.

Who was Alexander Fleming?

Alexander Fleming was a Scottish farmer's son born in 1881. He moved to London when he was 13 and later trained to be a doctor. During his training he developed an interest in bacteriology – the study of bacteria. During World War 1 he became an army doctor and carried on his work in France, where he was able to study the effects of bacteria on the wounds of the soldiers.

Alexander Fleming, 1881–1955

Alexander Fleming

Alexander Fleming's laboratory at St Mary's Hospital Paddington, London, 1928

Fleming's discovery

In 1928 Fleming was a research assistant investigating how bacteria cause diseases. His laboratory was cluttered with dishes in which he was growing cultures (small samples) of the bacteria he was working on. One day he noticed that one of the dishes was covered in mould. Most people would have thrown it away as a spoiled experiment, but Fleming decided to take a closer look. He saw that where the mould was growing, the bacteria had stopped developing.

The bacteria in the dish were those which turned wounds and cuts septic. One of Fleming's colleagues identified the mould as penicillin. Fleming did some experiments that tested the penicillin on animals and he found that it had no ill effects. After this he went back to work on his other research, leaving the development of penicillin to other people, in particular Howard Florey.

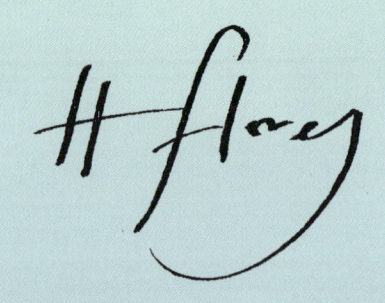

Who was Howard Florey?

Howard Florey was born in Adelaide, Australia, in 1898. He went to Adelaide University to study medicine, but in 1921 he moved to London to continue his studies. He became a professor at Oxford University in 1935.

In 1945 Florey was awarded the **Nobel Prize** for Medicine, which he shared with Alexander Fleming and Ernst Chain, for the development of penicillin.

Howard Florey, 1898-1968

Howard Florey

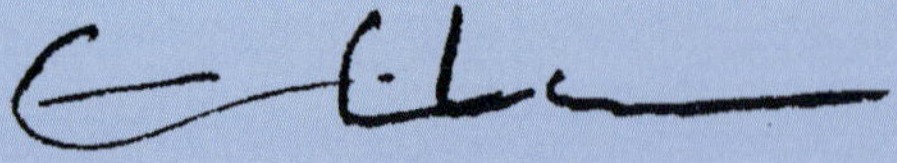

Ernst Chain

Ernst Chain, 1906-1979

Florey's work

Florey read about Fleming's work and decided to do more research into the effects of penicillin. He began work with Ernst Chain and, by 1940, their team had found a way of purifying penicillin and were able to test it on people.

When World War II started, there was suddenly a desperate need for penicillin, which was powerful and fast acting. Florey and Chain were not able to produce enough of it and had to ask the Americans to help. By the end of World War II, sufficient penicillin was being produced for it to be sold and used worldwide.

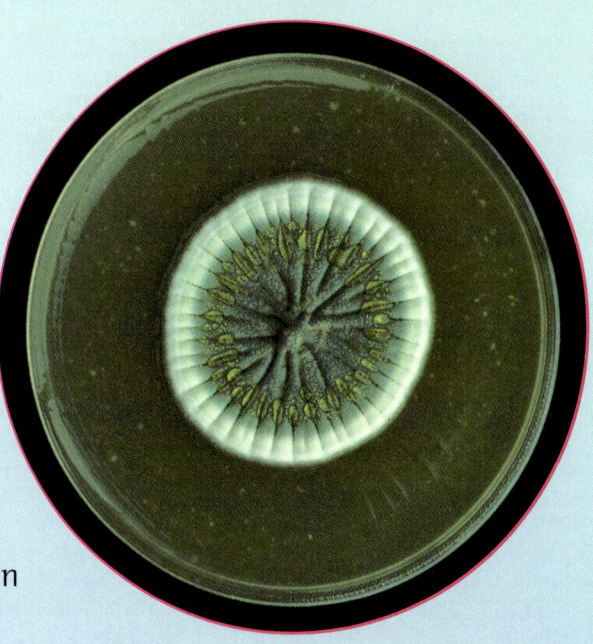

Penicillium fungus growing in a culture dish

Florey and Chain's process

The two scientists knew that the penicillin mould could be a very important substance if it could be made in large enough quantities to be supplied to lots of people.

The first thing Florey and Chain needed to do was to find out the best way to grow penicillin. They started by growing it in conditions that they controlled, so that they could find out which conditions suited it best. Samples of penicillin were grown in different **culture mediums**.

Other fungi cultures growing in petri dishes

Scientist at work, 1955

Secondly, Florey and Chain had to test the penicillin on different types of known bacteria. These tests are called trials, and the scientists watched these trials carefully. They noted down what happened to the bacteria and how long it took the penicillin to stop the bacteria growing.

The next step was to produce penicillin in a form that could be used easily to treat people. At this time, the penicillin they produced did not live long. They worked on a procedure to make a more purified and concentrated form of penicillin.

It was fairly easy to use penicillin on bacteria samples in a laboratory, but the scientists soon wanted to test their product on animals, and eventually on people. Once they had the more purified and concentrated form of penicillin they were ready to start this testing. They discovered that the penicillin killed harmful bacteria but was not harmful to animals or people.

In the USA, during the early 1940s scientists discovered ways of growing large enough quantities of penicillin to supply it to many people.

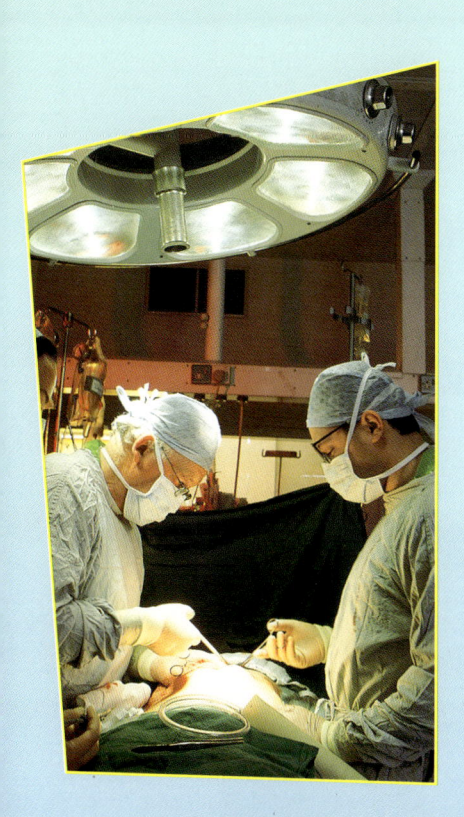

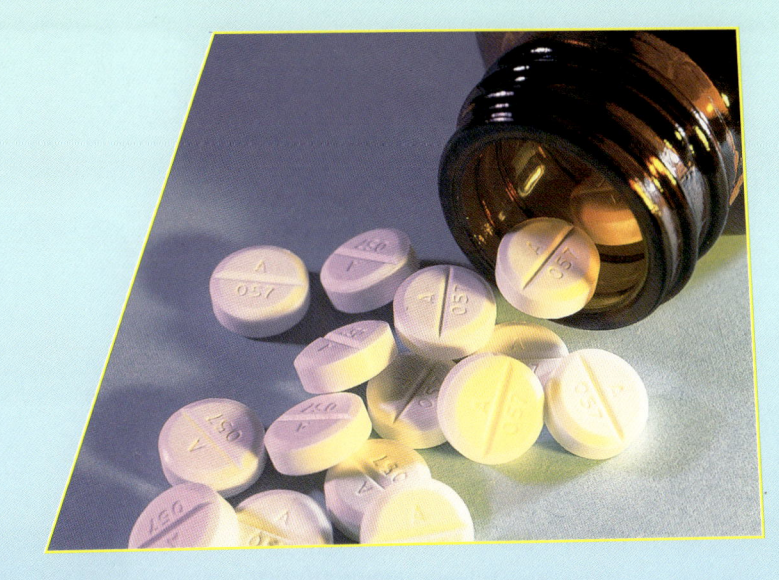

The importance of the discovery

The development of penicillin, and many other antibiotics based on moulds, has saved millions of lives throughout the world. Diseases which once wiped out vast numbers of people can now be controlled.

The process today

Huge quantities of antibiotics are 'grown' under carefully controlled conditions and produced in forms that can be given easily to patients. Scientists are developing new forms of antibiotics all the time. This is vital, as bacteria can change. The weakest bacteria are killed first, leaving the very strongest to grow, and these bacteria can gradually become **resistant** to antibiotics.

An experiment you could try

How to grow mould

You will need:
- A slice of bread
- A small clear plastic bag

What you have to do:
- Dampen your hand *slightly*. DO NOT wash your hand.

- Press your hand firmly onto the slice of bread and leave it there for 30 seconds.

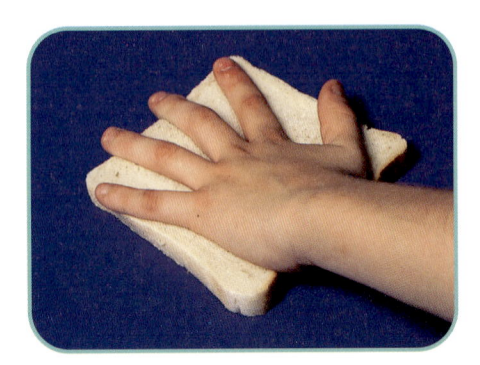

- Put the slice of bread into the plastic bag and seal the bag carefully.

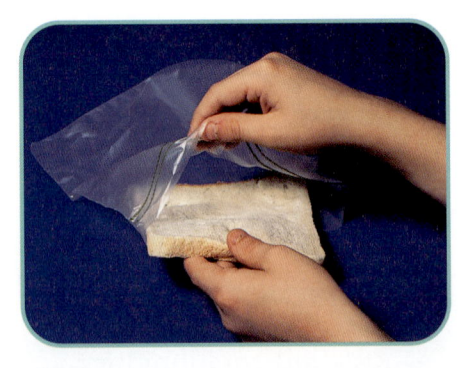

♦ Put the bag, with the handprint side of the bread facing upwards, onto a plate.

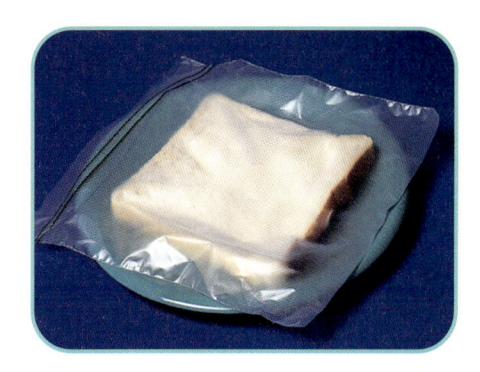

♦ Place the plate in a warm place, such as a windowsill or shelf in a warm room.

What to look for:
Watch for signs of mould growing on the bread.

An explanation:
Our hands, and in fact most parts of our bodies, often have mould spores on the skin. When you press your hand onto the slice of bread, some of these spores are transferred to the bread.

The bread is a good culture medium for the mould which can grow in the conditions provided by the plastic bag. This shows that we have lots of spores on our hands and that they grow well in certain conditions.

How heavy?

Why do things fall towards the floor? How is it that we don't float up into the air like a balloon when we jump? What keeps everything on the Earth from spinning off into space at a million miles an hour? These are questions that have been debated by scientists for many years. The answer is **gravity** – the **force** that keeps our feet on the ground and the Earth in its orbit. The first person to study gravity in a scientific way was Sir Isaac Newton.

Isaac Newton

Isaac Newton, 1642-16

Who was Isaac Newton?

Isaac Newton was born in England on Christmas Day, 1642. When he was 12, Isaac went to the local grammar school where he was placed in the bottom class. He was frustrated in this class and decided to prove that he was a better student than his teachers thought. He showed how clever he was by creating many different weird and wonderful inventions. One of these was a machine he could ride to school instead of walking. It was a four-wheeled vehicle that ran by a crank which he turned to make it go!

Isaac Newton

Newton's discovery

Isaac began studying at Cambridge University in 1661. He concentrated his studies on maths, which became such an obsession for him that he often forgot to eat and sometimes even to sleep! In the summer of 1665, while Isaac was still at Cambridge, a great disaster descended on many parts of England, including Cambridge itself – **The Great Plague**. The university was forced to close down and send its students home.

It was while at home, watching apples fall to the ground in the orchard, that Newton really began wondering why things fall straight to Earth, and not upwards or sideways.

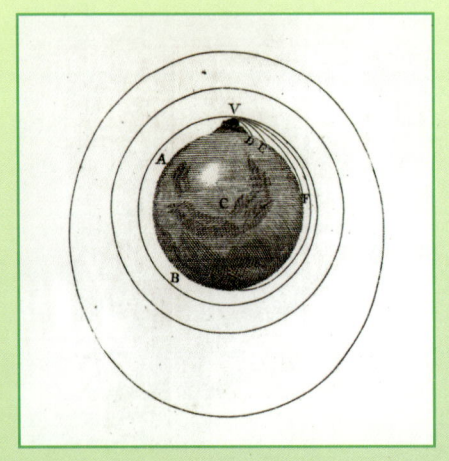

Engraving, by Isaac Newton, showing the effect of gravitational force on a rotating ball

In 1687 Isaac published a book that would become world famous. It contained many new ideas about how the Universe works. One of these ideas was Newton's Law of Gravity. It explained why things have weight. The idea was simply that everything in the Universe is pulled towards everything else. The Earth attracts us towards it, and this downward force, gravity, explains our weight.

Newton's process

As soon as Newton had seen the apples falling to the ground, he set to work to find out more. He started by looking at how quickly different things fell to Earth. He began by dropping objects of differing weights from the same height and recording these results. He noticed that the larger the weight, the quicker the object fell. He then kept increasing the height from which the same objects were dropped, and again recorded the results.

Newton applied his knowledge of maths to look at the relationship between the weight of the objects, the time it took these objects to fall to earth and the height from which they were dropped. It was with experiments such as this that Newton really began to formulate his ideas about gravity.

The significance of the discovery

The next time you weigh yourself, look at the reading of your weight and say, "The Earth is pulling me downwards with a force that is my weight". Newton also said that the force of gravity depends on the **mass** of the object doing the pulling. We know that the Earth has a much greater mass than the Moon.

Therefore, everything would be lighter on the Moon as the Moon's **gravitational pull** is less than that of Earth's. An object has the same mass on Earth and on the Moon, but weighs less on the Moon. That is why astronauts have to wear heavily weighted clothing to keep themselves steady on the Moon's surface and not go floating off into space when they jump.

Since Newton discovered the principle of gravity, forces are measured in **Newtons**. There are many forces that we come across every day – forces are exerted when we open cupboards and drawers, kick a football and run on the playing field. Weight is a force, so it too is measured in Newtons (N).

Here is a table showing the typical weights of some animals in Newtons. As you can see from the table, the larger the weight, the bigger the pull of gravity.

Animal	Weight
Mouse	1 N
Cat	30 N
Adult Woman	600 N
Adult Man	700 N
Blue Whale	2 000 000 N

Scientists have used Newton's Laws of Gravity in the pursuit of space travel. Without the ideas that Newton discovered about forces and gravity, astronauts would not be travelling in space or landing on the Moon.

An experiment you could try

Working out weights in Newtons

You should do this experiment with the help of an experienced adult.

You will need:
- A number of different objects found in the classroom
- A forcemeter

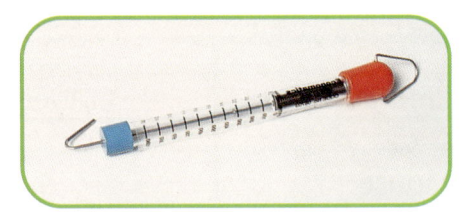

What you have to do:
- Weigh all of the objects on the forcemeter in kilograms (kg). Convert the weight into Newtons (N) (1kg = 10N).

- Write your answers down in a table like this:

Object name	Weight (in kilograms)	Weight in Newtons

More interesting calculations

♦ On the Moon, a 1kg object would weigh 1.5N. How much would your chosen objects weigh?

♦ Write your answers down in a table like this:

Object name	Weight (in kilograms)	Weight in Newtons

♦ Objects weigh twice as much on Jupiter as they do on Earth, where 1kg = I0N. What do you think your objects would weigh on Jupiter?

Radioactive reactions

Until the very end of the 19th century, no one had the faintest idea that some **elements** lose very tiny specks of matter, or particles. Now that we know this, we say that these substances are radioactive. As radioactive elements slowly lose the particles that are shooting out of them, they transform into other elements.

The first person to discover that some elements are radioactive was the French scientist Henri Becquerel and, like many great discoveries, it happened by accident! Becquerel had placed some photographic plates (like modern camera film) next to a sample of rock he had collected containing the radioactive element **uranium**. When the photographic plates were developed, they had turned completely black, exactly what would have happened if they had been exposed to the light. Becquerel realized that something from the uranium must have affected the photographic plates.

Antoine-Henri Bequerel, 1852–1908

Becquerel's discovery became the life work of two other scientists, Marie Curie and her husband Pierre. They developed a procedure for separating **radium** from a substance called pitchblende, which is an **ore** of uranium.

Henri Becquer

Marie Curie

Who was Marie Curie?

Marie Sklodowska was born in Warsaw, Poland, in 1867. Her mother was the principal of a girl's boarding school and her father was a professor of maths and physics. Marie was very clever, but at that time, girls in Poland were not allowed to attend university. So in 1891 she went to Paris, France, to study. She was a brilliant and hard-working student and she obtained degrees in both physics and maths. She also met her future husband, Pierre Curie, while studying in Paris. They were married in 1895 and began to work together.

Marie Curie, 1867–1934

Pierre Curie

Pierre Curie, 1859–1906

Marie Curie's discoveries

Marie tested a lot of different substances, looking for effects similar to the ones Becquerel had discovered. She tested a substance called pitchblende until, after a lot of hard work, she and Pierre discovered a new element that she named polonium, after her native country, Poland.

Marie discovered that the pitchblende was more radioactive than she first thought. It was even more radioactive than the pure uranium that could be extracted from it. She thought this must mean that there was another element in the pitchblende. She decided to try to separate this other element from the pitchblende.

Working with Pierre, she used tonnes of pitchblende and eventually they **isolated** radium.

The process of extracting pure radium from the pitchblende began in 1899. It took nearly four years of work, but in 1902 they produced 0.1g of the pure element.

Black uranite

Pitchblende

A pellet of plutonium

A "button" of uranium

24

Marie and Pierre Curie in a laboratory

Marie Curie's process

Marie Curie used a particular method to isolate radium from pitchblende. She and her husband had tonnes and tonnes of pitchblende delivered to their workshop. This material was not pure pitchblende but contained all sorts of other stones and soil, so the first thing they had to do was **sift** the pitchblende to remove all of this other material.

As soon as they had enough pitchblende to begin working on, they ground it to a fine powder.

Next, the powder was boiled up with a substance called soda. This made the pitchblende separate into two parts, one solid and one liquid.

The liquid was thrown away and the remaining solid material carefully collected.

By this time only a small amount of solid was left. They had to dissolve the solid material in acid before they could move on to the next stage of the process.

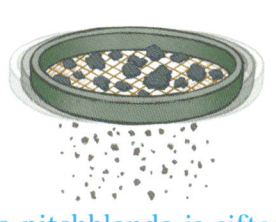

the pitchblende is sifted

the pitchblende is ground to a powder

the powdered pitchblende is mixed with soda and boiled

a solid is produced

the solid is separated from the liquid, and the liquid is discarded

the solid matter is gathered

the solid matter is mixed with acid

The experiment illustrated below shows, in a simple way, the sort of process a scientist will use to separate chemicals.

Atoms will combine to make molecules.

A new substance is added which makes the atoms recombine.

The Curies had to remove, one by one, all the elements that they knew were in the pitchblende to find the element that they were looking for. They were able to do this using chemicals, because they knew that each of the elements would react with a different chemical, so they could find it and remove it. Once they had removed all of the elements they knew were in the pitchblende, they could see if there was anything left.

As the sample got smaller with each element that was removed, the level of radioactivity increased.

Finally, after they had removed all the elements that they knew were contained in pitchblende, there was still something left – the unknown element.

They named this radium.

The new compound can be extracted by **filtering** or evaporation.

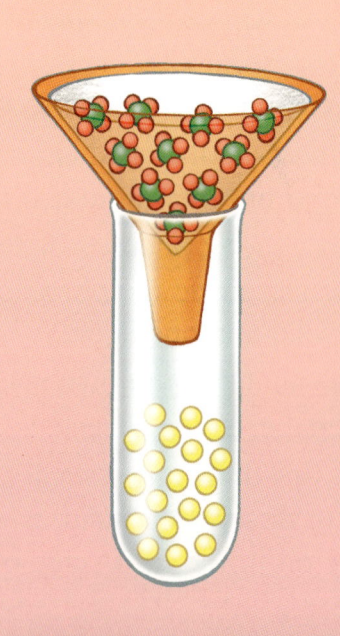

Radium is so radioactive that it makes other things radioactive as well. Nowadays, all Marie's notebooks still have to be kept in a lead-lined vault because they are so dangerous.

The significance of the discovery

The particles that come shooting out of radioactive elements make energy called radioactivity. The discovery of radioactivity has had an enormous effect on science and on our everyday lives.

The energy given off by radioactive elements can be used in medicine to kill dangerous cancer cells in the body or to take X-rays.

Heat can be produced by carefully controlling the energy given off by radioactive materials, and this heat can be used to produce electricity in power stations.

Radioactivity can even be used in archaeology. All living things contain a substance called carbon. After their death, the amount of radioactivity in the carbon slowly decreases. By measuring the amount of radioactivity found in the carbon of something that was once living, its age can be worked out.

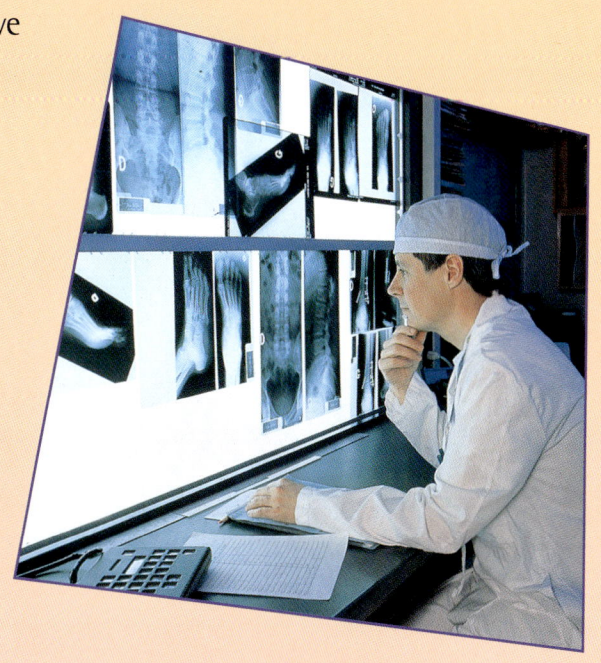

Sellafield nuclear power station in Cumbria, England

Bikini Atoll in the Pacific Marshall Islands, 1946, atom bomb test

Although radioactivity has brought many benefits, there are risks. If the energy from radioactive substances is released in an uncontrolled way, there can be a huge explosion, and this process is used to make **nuclear weapons**. As well as the danger of explosions, the radioactivity itself is harmful to the body, even in very small quantities.

These days we know how dangerous radioactivity is, but the Curies had no idea of the risks when they were carrying out their work. They both became very ill as a result of radiation poisoning, but they still continued with their work.

The process today

The process developed by the Curies of **refining** radioactive elements is still used today. However, it is much more complex, and done by machines to ensure safety. Scientists are now also able to produce new radioactive elements not found in nature.

An experiment you could try

How to separate salt from a mixture of sand, salt and water
You should do this experiment with the help of an experienced adult.

You will need:
- 25 g of kitchen salt
- 50 g of dry fine sand
- 100 ml of water
- an electric kettle
- a coffee filter or thin piece of clean cloth, such as muslin

What you have to do:
- Mix the sand and salt together and put the mixture into a container.

- Heat the water until it boils.

- Pour the water into the sand/salt mixture and stir well.

Separating the mixture:
- Filter the mixture by pouring it through a coffee filter or a piece of clean thin cloth into another container (the filters from a coffee machine are good for this). The sand will remain in the filter while the liquid, containing the dissolved salt, will pass through into the container.

EXPERIMENT ◆ EXPERIMENT

♦ Leave the sand to dry.

♦ Pour the liquid (water and salt mixture) into a shallow container.

♦ Allow the solution to evaporate by leaving the container in a warm place, such as a window sill or shelf in a warm room.

♦ After all the water has gone, you will be left with crystals of pure salt.

An explanation:

The process you have used is very similar to the process used by the Curies to isolate radium. You have used everyday substances. They were working with dangerous substances, but the scientific procedures used are the same.

Glossary

antibiotics the name given to a special group of medicines that fight infection caused by bacteria

bacteria germs

culture medium something that contains the right mixture of foods needed for growing bacteria, and used for this purpose

elements a chemical substance in its purest form

filter to separate a liquid from a solid by pouring the mixture through a material that will allow the liquid to drain through, but will leave the solid behind

force the effect on objects by pushing or pulling them

gravitational pull the amount of force which attracts objects to each other

gravity a force in nature that acts as an attraction between objects

Great Plague, The a plague that was introduced into Britain by fleas on rats arriving in ships from the Far East in 1665. Often called the Black Death, over 100 000 people died in London alone.

isolate to separate one thing from other things

mass the amount of matter in an object

Newtons the common unit of measurement of force

Nobel Prize a prize awarded annually from a fund established by Alfred Bernhard Nobel, to be given to people who have made a difference to humanity

nuclear weapons weapons that get their power from very radioactive materials

ore rock or earth from which metal can be obtained

radium a highly radioactive element

refine to remove all the impurities from a substance

resistant not affected by something

septic a wound that is septic has become seriously infected by bacteria

sift to pass a powdery substance through a sieve to remove the lumps

uranium a radioactive element

Index

A	antibiotics	6, 11
	astronauts	18
B	bacteria	6, 7, 8, 10, 11
	Becquerel, Henri	22, 24
C	carbon	27
	Chain, Ernst	8, 9–10
	Curie, Marie	22–26, 28, 30
	Curie, Pierre	22–26, 28, 30
D	diphtheria	6
E	elements	22, 24, 26, 27, 28
F	Fleming, Alexander	6–8
	Florey, Howard	8–10
G	gravity	14, 16, 17
J	Jupiter	21
M	mould	7, 12, 13
N	Newton, Isaac	14–19
	Newtons (measure of force)	19, 20, 21
	Newton's Law of Gravity	16, 19
	Nobel Prize	8
	nuclear weapons	28
P	penicillin	8, 9, 10, 11, 27–28
	pitchblende	22, 24, 25, 26
	polonium	24
R	radioactivity	22, 24, 26, 27, 28
	radium	22, 24, 25, 26, 30
T	typhoid	6
U	uranium	22, 24
W	weight	16–21
X	X-rays	27